Cheetahs

Kate Riggs

CREATIVE EDUCATION

seedlings

Published by Creative Education
P.O. Box 227, Mankato, Minnesota 56002
Creative Education is an imprint of
The Creative Company
www.thecreativecompany.us

Design and production by Ellen Huber
Art direction by Rita Marshall
Printed in the United States of America

Photographs by Corbis (Paul A. Souders), Getty Images (Martin Harvey, Michael K. Nichols), iStockphoto (Hilton Kotze), Shutterstock (Mark Beckwith, Neil Burton, Eric Isselee, Stu Porter, Ian Rentoul, Radovan Spurny, Valdecasas, Vishnevskiy Vasily, Albie Venter)

Library of Congress Cataloging-in-Publication Data
Riggs, Kate.
Cheetahs / Kate Riggs.
p. cm. — (Seedlings)
Includes bibliographical references and index.
Summary: A kindergarten-level introduction to cheetahs, covering their growth process, behaviors, the lands they call home, and such defining physical features as their spotted fur.
ISBN 978-1-60818-452-1
1. Cheetah—Juvenile literature. I. Title.

QL737.C23R538 2014
599.75'9—dc23 2013029065

CCSS: RI.K.1, 2, 3, 4, 5, 6, 7;
RI.1.1, 2, 3, 4, 5, 6, 7; RF.K.1, 3; RF.1.1

9 8 7 6 5 4 3

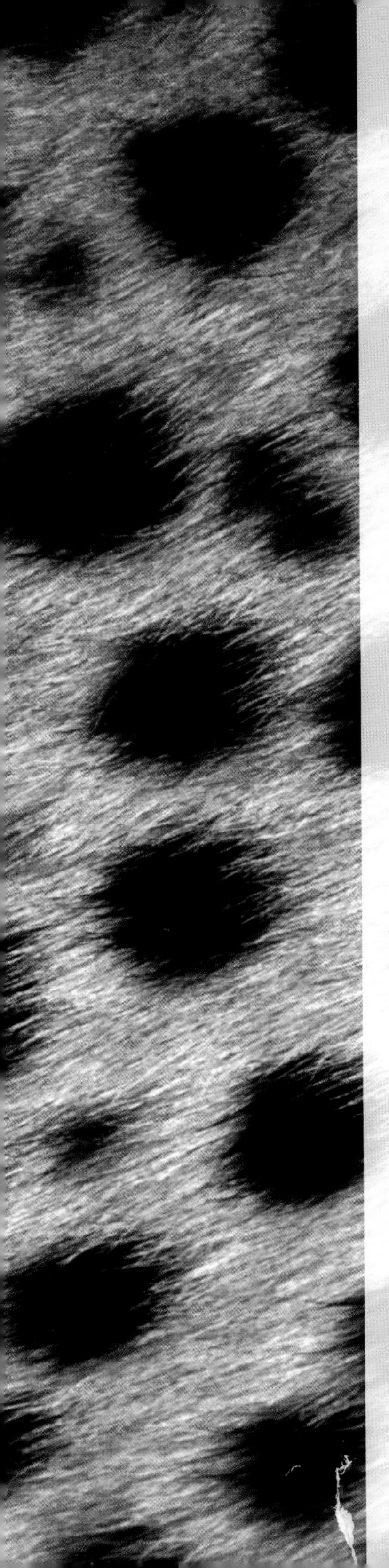

TABLE OF CONTENTS

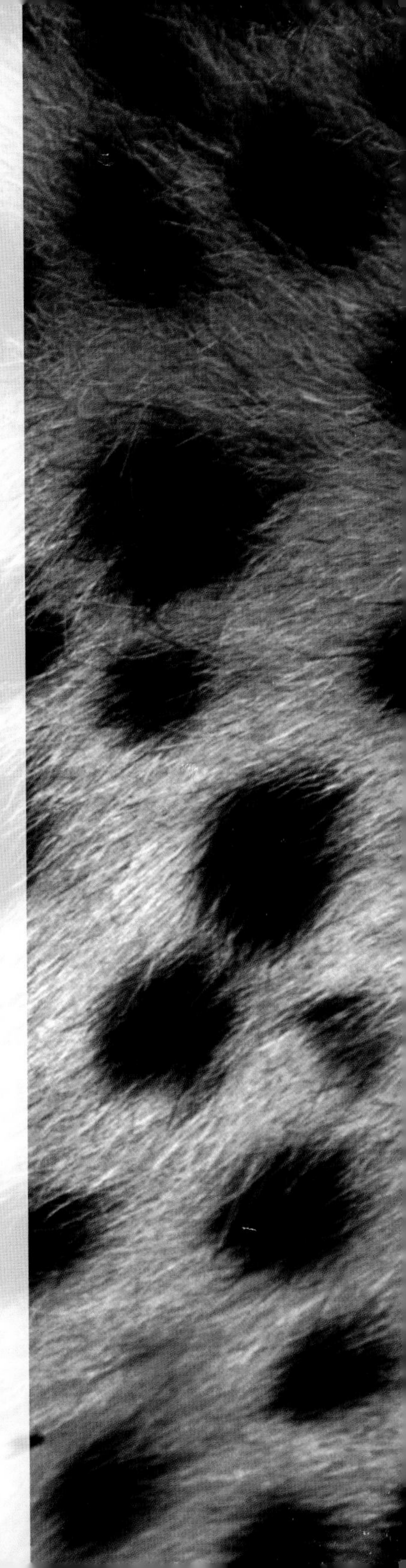

Hello, cheetahs!

Cheetahs are fast cats.

They live in
Africa and Iran.

Cheetahs have spotted fur.
The spots are black.

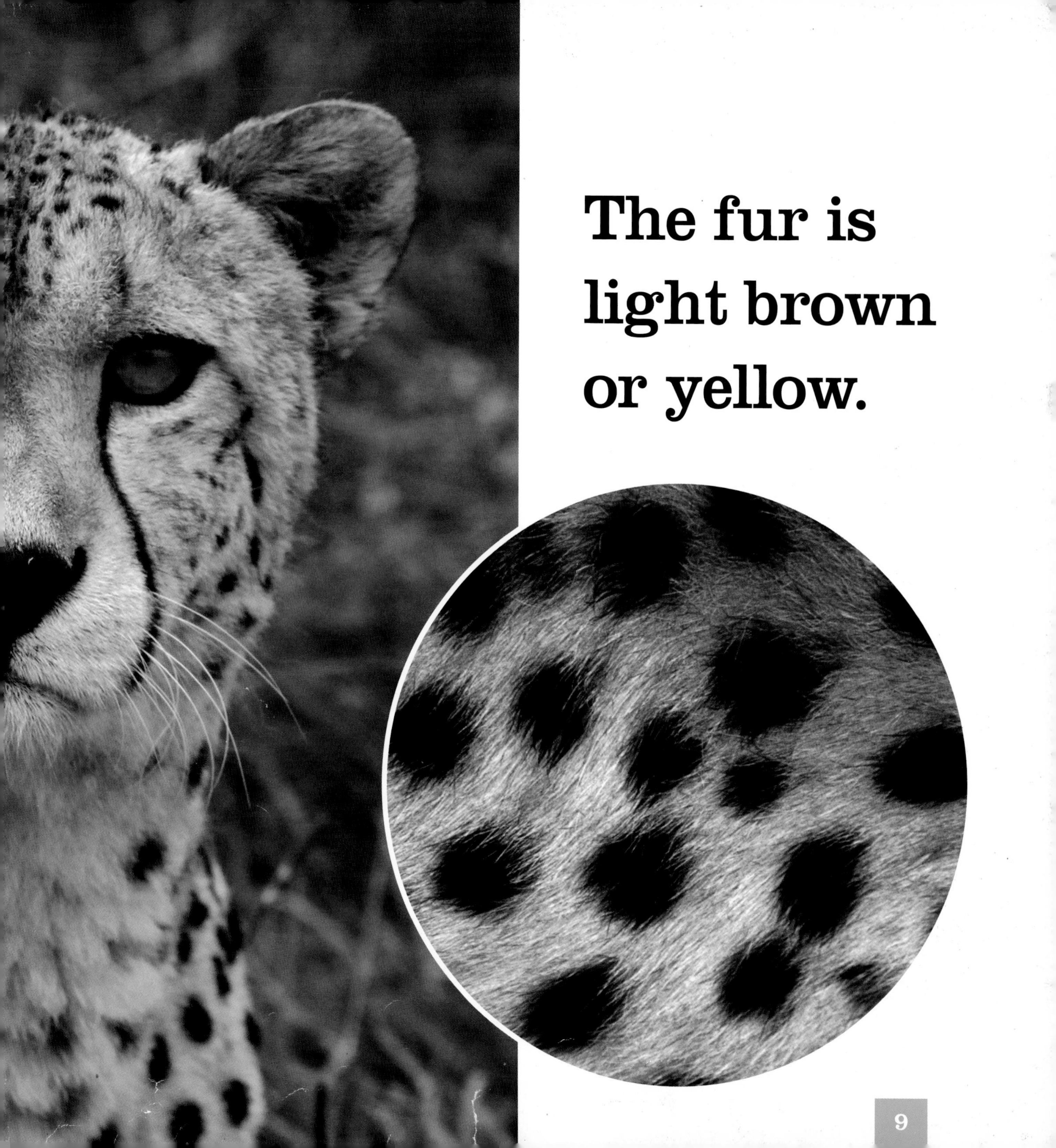

The fur is light brown or yellow.

Cheetahs have black tear lines on their face.

They have long tails.

Cheetahs eat meat.
They chase antelopes.

Sometimes they eat hares.

A baby cheetah is called a cub. Cubs live with their mother.

cheetahs live in groups.

Cubs like to play.

Adult cheetahs look for food. They rest when it is too hot to hunt.

Goodbye, cheetahs!

Picture a Cheetah

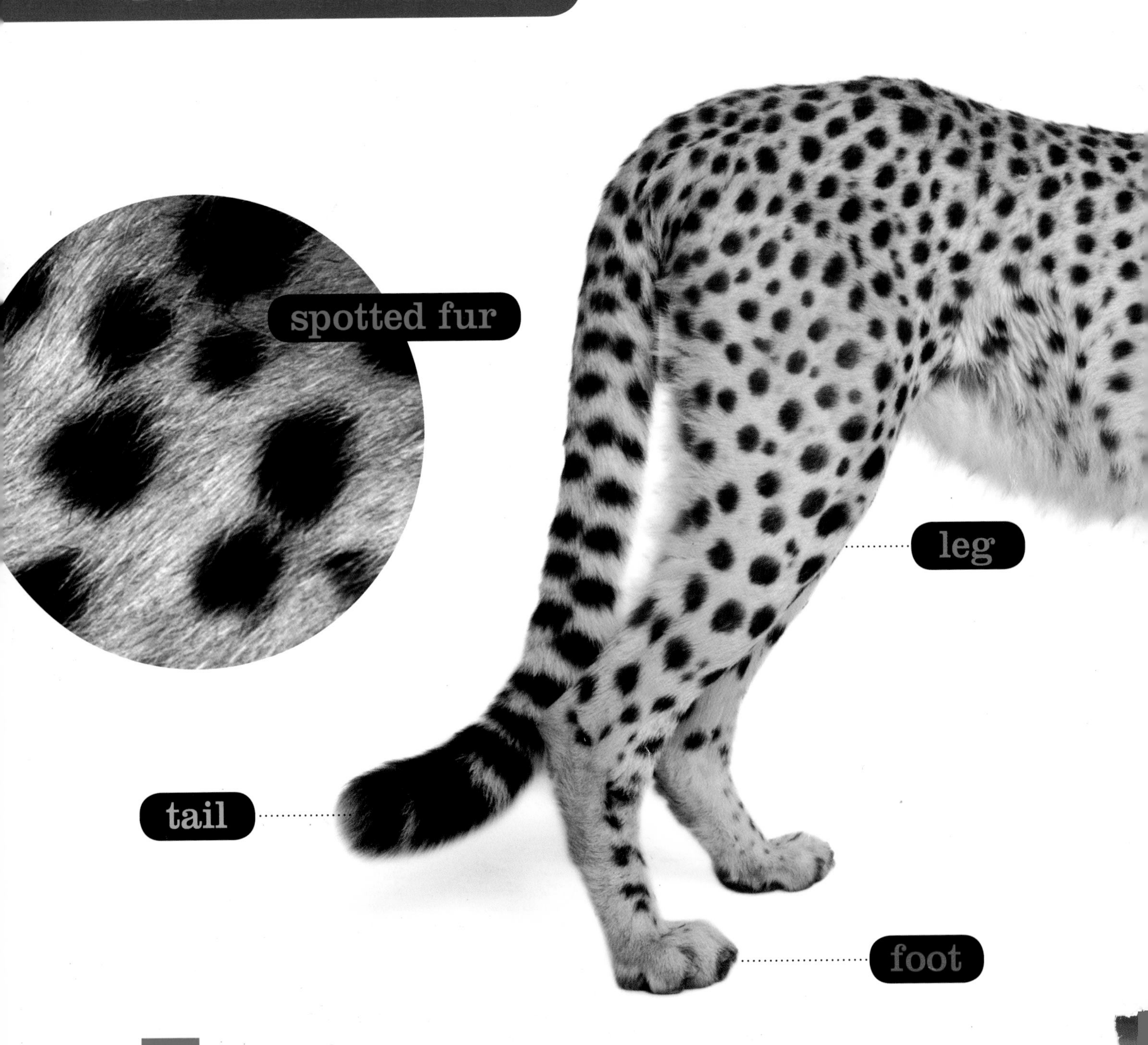

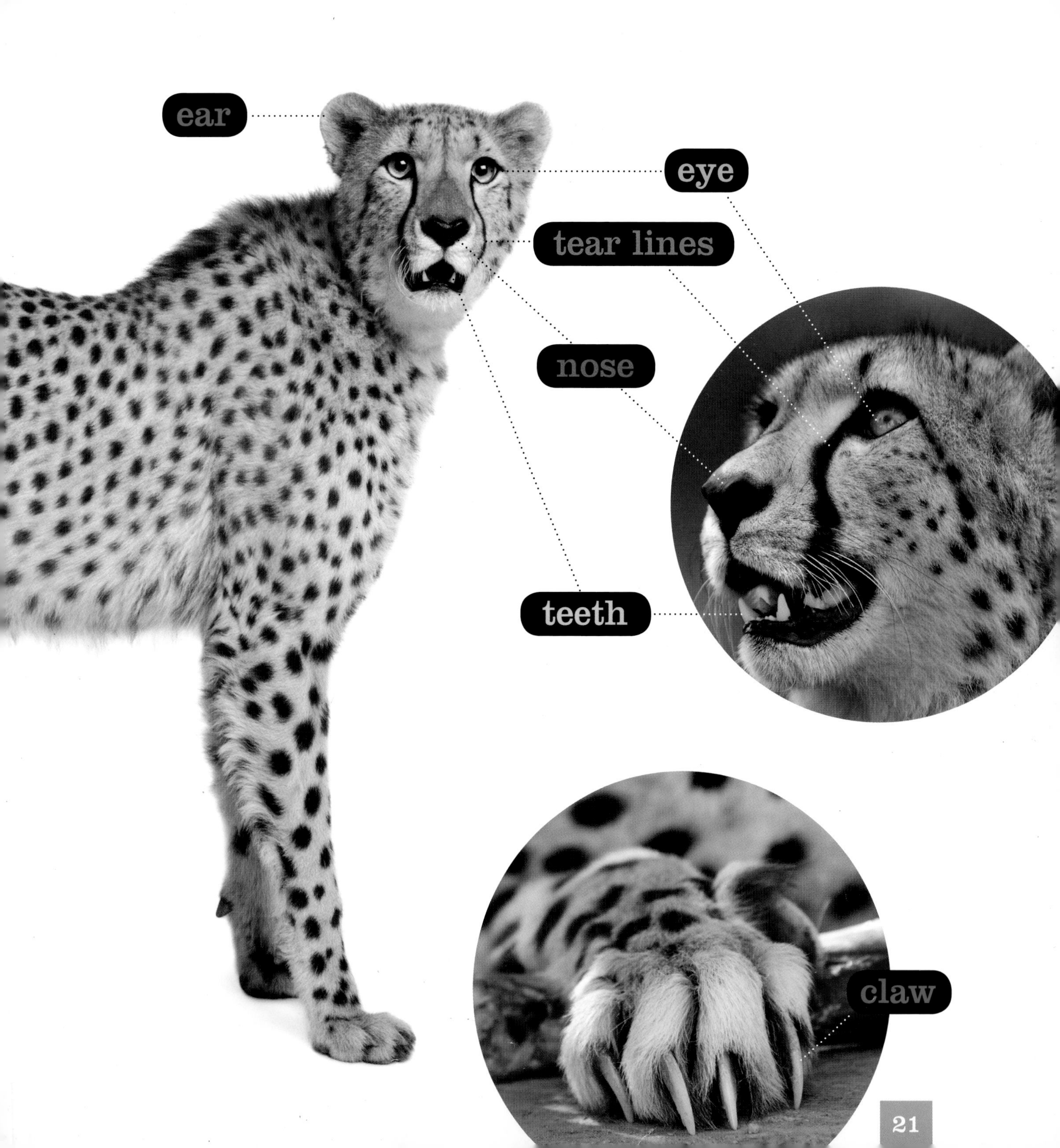
ear
eye
tear lines
nose
teeth
claw

Words to Know

Africa: the second-biggest piece of land in the world

fur: the short, hairy coat of an animal

hares: rabbit-like animals that live in Africa

tear lines: black markings on the fur of a cheetah's face

Read More

Johns, Chris, and Elizabeth Carney. *Face to Face with Cheetahs.* Washington, D.C.: National Geographic Society, 2008.

Marsh, Laura. *Cheetahs.* Washington, D.C.: National Geographic Society, 2011.

Websites

Cheetah Cub Craft
http://www.dltk-kids.com/crafts/cartoons/thornberrys/mcheetah.htm
Make your own cheetah cub with a few materials.

Printable Cheetah Mask
http://www.freekidscrafts.com/printable_cheetah_mask-e1804.html
Make a mask, and pretend to be a cheetah!

Note: Every effort has been made to ensure that the websites listed above are suitable for children, that they have educational value, and that they contain no inappropriate material. However, because of the nature of the Internet, it is impossible to guarantee that these sites will remain active indefinitely or that their contents will not be altered.

Index